God
Invented
Sex

God Invented Sex

An Interactive Guide to Sexual Purity

LISA GORDON, MSW

God Invented Sex: An Interactive Guide to Sexual Purity
by Lisa Gordon

Cover Design by Atinad Designs.

© Copyright 2016

SAINT PAUL PRESS, DALLAS, TEXAS

First Printing, 2016

ISBN-10: 1534935878

ISBN-13: 978-1534935877

Printed in the U.S.A.

contents

foreword

God Invented Sex: An Interactive Guide to Sexual Purity is the journey of Lisa's discovery of the power of purity and the importance that purity plays in the life of the believer. She takes you back to the beginning of her journey through her struggles to find the very essence of how our sexual choices can camouflage what we see as love. *God Invented Sex* reclaims who the Creator and Inventor of sex really is and what He intended and purposed for this great invention. The late Dr. Myles Monroe once said, "If you don't know the purpose of a thing, abuse is inevitable." We have seen in our culture, today, that there has been no limit to repercussions of sexual promiscuity including broken homes, teenage pregnancy, and an increase in sexually transmitted diseases. As a result, abuse is evident as we see the unimaginable being lived out before us through movies, videos, media, and even in our churches. Is what we see really God's plan for sex, or have we highjacked this wonderful creation of His for our own pleasure?

Lisa pulls no punches as she gives readers a peek into her personal struggles with sex and how it impacted the choices she made. She reveals in the vernacular of the day why so many people struggle emotionally in relationships, and that is because they do not understand God's true intentions for sexual purity. Lisa is one of my spiritual daughters, and I have watched her grow into a wonderful woman of God. Her heart to serve others is evident to everyone who knows her. As a pastor, I see all too often the negative impact that sexual promiscuity has on teens, as well as on unmarried and married adults. Even in the church, we have failed to articulate the power of sexual purity as Lisa has done in this interactive guide to sexual purity. This book was an eye opener to me and has given me a more passionate reason to proclaim this truth, and it is that God invented sex.

Dr. Dale E. Wafer, Senior Pastor
DC City Church in Washington, DC.

introduction

I want to wait, but I don't know how.

I'm tired of giving myself sexually and feeling so empty afterwards.

I feel so out of control.

I want to stop, but I can't!

Why do I feel so empty?

I feel like pieces of me are being chipped away.

Ohhh, I can't wait to get a piece of that! Ummm.

I'm so tired of allowing people to use and abuse me and my body for their pleasure, what about me?

I think I have an STD.

My period is 5 days late.

Can you relate to any of the above? News flash everyone: contrary to popular belief, God created sex! And that goes for Trey Songz, Mr. "I Invented Sex." Sex is nothing to be ashamed of. It's not a sin. It's something that we should feel free to talk about. It is something that God created as a gift to give us great pleasure and satisfaction when used appropriately. It was also created as a vehicle to bring two people who love each other together in unity and to allow them to not only connect in a physical, mental, and emotional way but also in a spiritual way. It's a way of connecting two souls and joining them together as one.

As we begin to explore the purpose of sex, we also need to evaluate the meaning of sexual purity. Sexual purity is a personal decision. It goes way beyond the physical act of not having sex; it is a lifestyle choice. It starts as a mental awareness and then leads to a physical process. Once we are able to control our minds by arming ourselves with knowledge, we are then able to make better choices and decisions. The Bible says, **For this is the will of God, your sanctification: that you abstain from sexual immorality; that each one of you know how to control his own body in holiness and honor, not in the passion of lust like the Gentiles who do not know God (1 Thessalonians 4:35 ESV)**. Sexual purity is really about controlling your own body by empowering your mind.

Some people believe that as long as they are not having sex, everything else is allowed. What's everything else? Everything else can be masturbation, kissing, oral sex, bumping and grinding (with clothes on or off), etc. I once felt that way, too. However, I have learned that as long as I continued to arouse my senses in any sexual capacity, the act would come sooner or later. If I was strong enough to delay the act, the emotional and mental exhaustion of wanting that need to be fulfilled after it was aroused could be downright painful, frustrating, and stressful. Most times the end result was inevitable and I was left thinking: "God knows my heart" or "God knows that it's too hard to abstain from sex" and off I went repeating the cycle. At some point, we have to choose to make wise decisions.

In this book, I want to look at various aspects of sex in an interactive way and share valuable tools for the single individual who desires to wait, stop, and/or maintain sexual purity until marriage. At the end of each chapter, I present questions that will promote critical thinking and personal reflection. This book is not meant to judge, preach at, or condemn anyone. It is simply a guide to maintaining sexual purity based on life lessons learned. I know sex is everywhere and it appears that everyone is DOING IT. However, I have found that there is still a remnant of people who have not given up on doing things God's way, including myself. Most people really want to make better decisions but just do not know how. Most people like myself are aware of the do's and the don'ts but just don't know how to stop. And for the rest of you who are not quite sure if you want to wait or stop, this book is for you also. There is no harm in receiving new information. There is no pressure. Read on and then you decide what's best for you. Just know in advance that we aren't sugar-coating anything. It's time to call a spade a spade. Okay? Let's go!

Current Statistics and Trends

Before we get started, it's important that we look at current statistics and trends on this topic. According to the Center for Disease Control and Prevention:

Among U.S. high school students surveyed in 2013

- 47% never had sexual intercourse.
- 34% had sexual intercourse during the previous 3 months, and, of these
- 41% did not use a condom the last time they had sex.
- Nearly 10,000 young people (aged 13-24) were diagnosed with HIV infection in the United States in 2013.
- Nearly half of the 20 million new STDs each year were among young people, between the ages of 15 to 24.
- Approximately 273,000 babies were born to teen girls aged 15–19 years in 2013.

"During the past three decades, the level of sexual activity in adolescents in the United States has increased." (Source: American Academy of Pediatrics)

Among teens each year, there are about 3 million cases of sexually transmitted diseases (STDs), and approximately 1 million pregnancies. Human immunodeficiency virus (HIV) infection is the sixth leading cause of death among persons aged 15-24 years in the United States. (Source: Centers for Disease Control, Atlanta, GA)

According to the American Academy of Pediatrics, 36.9 percent of 14-year-olds have had sex; this is more than one out of three. Among 12th graders, 66.4 percent have had sex.

References

1. CDC. "Youth Risk Behavior Surveillance—United States, 2013. *MMWR* 2014;63(SS-4).
2. CDC. "Diagnoses of HIV infection and AIDS in the United States and dependent areas, 2013. *HIV Surveillance Report*, Volume 25.
3. Satterwhite CL, et al. "Sexually transmitted infections among U.S. women and men: Prevalence and incidence estimates, 2008. *Sexually Transmitted Diseases*, 2013; 40(3): pp. 187-193.
4. Martin JA, Hamilton BE, Osterman MJK, Curtin SC, Mathews TJ. Births: final data for 2013. *National Vital Statistics Report*. 2015; 64 (1).

Sexual Activity

A recent study reveals that 88 % of unmarried young adults (ages 18-29) are having sex. The same study, conducted by The National Campaign to Prevent Teen and Unplanned Pregnancy, reveals the number does not drop much among Christians. Of those surveyed who self-identify as "evangelical," 80 percent say they have had sex.

Pregnancy

According to the Guttmacher Institute, nearly half of all pregnancies in America are unintended. And of those, 40 percent end in abortion.

Abstinence

According to Waitingtillmarriage.com:
- About 3% of Americans waited until marriage to have sex (successfully).
- 3% of the population equates to 10 million people who waited until marriage for sex.

The results of a study conducted by the National Institute of Child Health and Human Development reported in 2004, that teenagers who watch a lot of television with sexual content are twice as likely to engage in sexual activity than those who watch few programs with sexual content. According to Rebecca Collins, the psychologist who headed the study, "This is the strongest evidence yet that the sexual content of television programs encourages adolescents to initiate sexual intercourse and other sexual activities." The study covered 1,792 adolescents between the ages of twelve and seventeen.

Key findings:
- Teens who watch a lot of television with sexual content are more likely to initiate intercourse in the

following year.

- Television in which characters talk about sex affects teens just as much as television that actually shows sexual activity.
- Shows that portray the risks of sex can help educate teens.

Source: Collins, Rebecca L., Marc N. Elliott, Sandra H. Berry, David E. Kanouse, Dale Kunkel, Sarah B. Hunter and Angela Miu, "Does Watching Sex on Television Influence Teens' Sexual Activity?", Santa Monica, Calif.: RAND Corporation, RB9068, 2004. As of August 18, 2015: http://www.rand.org/pubs/research_briefs/RB9068

Similarly, a study conducted by the University of North Carolina which covered 1,017 adolescents between the ages of twelve to fourteen and then again two years later, reported in 2006, that those exposed to the highest levels of sexual content in music, magazines, television, and movies became more sexually active. According to Jane Brown, the chief author of the report, "This is the first time we've shown that the more kids are exposed to sex in media the earlier they have sex." Neither study included exposure to the Internet.

Source: Article: Sexy Media Matter: Exposure to Sexual Content in Music, Movies, Television, and Magazines Predicts Black and White Adolescents' Sexual Behavior. Authors: Jane D. Brown, PhD, MA; Kelly Ladin L'Engle, PhD, MPH; Carol J. Pardun, PhD, MA; Guang Guo, PhD; Kristin Kenneavy, MA; Christine Jackson, PhD, MA. PEDIATRICS Vol. 117 No. 4 April 1, 2006; pp. 1018-1027; (doi: 10.1542/peds.2005-1406)

The Family Research Council reported a study showing that people who strongly believe in restricting the sexual relationship to marriage end up nearly *twice* as likely to view their sexual relations to be satisfying as do those who don't oppose sexual relations outside of marriage [72% compared to 41% - *Family Policy*, 2/1994].

Do Not Awaken Love Until It's Time

Daughters of Jerusalem, I charge you: Do not arouse or awaken love until it so desires.
(Song of Solomon 8:4, NIV)

I remember being in 7th grade and running around with my friends saying, "No ring, No thing!" I was a loud young lady and always very passionate about my stance or cause. Although I did not attend church consistently throughout my early life, I did have phases where I would attend more consistently than others. One thing is certain, I never questioned God's existence. I knew He was real and I believed what I read about Him in the Bible. I remember days of looking in the sky and wondering when would the world end or even being consumed at times with not wanting to go to hell. The thought of burning forever and ever was not something that I wanted to experience. Looking back, though,

I always remember hearing His voice. Hey, all I can say is that in 7th grade, life was good. I loved the Lord, loved my friends and was determined to live my life for Christ which included not having sex until marriage.

Somewhere beyond that point, I fell off from attending church like I used to. I was more interested in hanging out with my friends, listening to music, and talking to and about the boys. I became "hot in the pants" and was really smelling myself. I started attracting the attention of boys and older men especially when I wore certain outfits. I would hear over and over again: 'You have a nice shape,' 'Girl, you got a big butt,' 'Man, do you have some beautiful legs,' 'You are sexy!' Oh, and did I mention that I loved music? R&B to be exact. By this time some of the best hits where Jodeci's *Forever My Lady* and *Come and Talk to Me*. I loved Tevin Campbell's *Can we Talk* and some R. Kelly, *Bump and Grind* (*I don't see nothing wrong, with a little bump and grind!*) Yikes! I would just sit with my Walkman singing my heart out for hours to the lyrics of these songs and just swaying to the beat. By the time 10th grade came around, 'No ring, No thing' was a slogan of the past and I was trying to get into something quick. It's kind of funny, because at some point, it really felt like something was driving me and my need of wanting to have sex. Even though I knew it was wrong, I wanted to do it more and more.

There was definitely something driving me and I did not know exactly what. It's easy to say it was the devil, but I was also making choices and decisions that did not make it easy for me to maintain sexual purity. I know we talk about teenage hormones, but it felt like there was so much more going on. I did not understand the power of music and its influence on the mind. I didn't understand that if I watched pornography, it would make it harder for me to fight these strong urges that were rising up in my body. There was just so much that I did not understand. Unfortunately, in my eyes, there was not a safe place to talk about these feelings and urges where I could receive helpful information. Being raised in a Caribbean family, it was a No-No to try to ask an adult about sex! That would be totally out of line. The most that we were expected to be concerned with at this point in our lives was God and getting a good education. Unfortunately, the only people who I could talk to were my peers, and most of them were in the same place as myself or had already started having sex. There were also feelings of shame and guilt because many of us heard in church that fornication was a sin. However, there was no one available to teach us how to live sexually pure lives once we walked outside of the church. As a result, everything was fair game and some of us (including myself) learned through trial and error.

Exercise

1. How many times in a day do you take in sexual images?

_____

_____

_____

_____

2. How does sex affect your 5 senses?

_____

_____

_____

_____

3. What is your honest stance on sexual purity?

_____

_____

_____

_____

That 3-Letter Word

Nevertheless, [to avoid] fornication, let every man have his own wife, and let every woman have her own husband.
(1 Corinthians 7:2, KJV)

Webster's Dictionary defines sex as an act performed with another for sexual gratification. It is also known as intercourse, lovemaking, mating, and sexual relations. Street terms for sex are bumping and grinding, screw, bang, sleeping with, friends with benefits, the wild thing, doing it, etc. How can something that feels so good be so wrong? Let's not forget to mention that sex, in some cases, can also be used as medicine to make one feel good or better. It can be used as a weapon to control others or used as a means to acquire finances and possessions. Some people use sex as a great divergent from having to deal with real issues (in some cases anger, hurt, grief, and pain). Who wants to deal with their issues and true feelings especially as a teen? At that age, most teens just want to have fun.

SEX is powerful. It enhances people's moods and emotions. A person may not be interested in an individual in the least but after having sex with that person may start to feel things and see things that might not necessarily be true. SEX can also influence you to abandon your goals and dreams. The draw of sexual energy or tension between two individuals can make one throw their values and morals out the window and succumb to filling that immediate need. SEX can be forced or it can be consensual. SEX is a word that most parents struggle to talk about. SEX is a word that most teens and young people want to know more about. SEX is the vehicle for creating life. SEX can be fulfilling. SEX can be painful. SEX can be memorable. Sex outside of marriage can be very dangerous.

Exercise

1. What are your thoughts on the purpose of sex?

_____

_____

_____

_____

2. What are some natural consequences of having sex before marriage?

_____

_____

_____

_____

3. What are some benefits to waiting for sex until marriage?

_____

_____

_____

_____

In All Your Getting, Get Understanding

Wisdom is the principal thing; therefore get wisdom: and with all thy getting get understanding.
(Proverbs 4:7, KJV)

Let's make this clear: sex in itself is not bad. This is something that I really want this generation to understand. It was created by the Lord for us to bring us great pleasure. I now look at the Father and say, 'Wow, Lord! You created this gift for us to enjoy.' There was nothing that we did or could do to come up with the idea of sex. It shows me just how much the Father loves us. We run into problems when we do not understand the purpose of sex. It's like giving a toddler keys to a brand new car. That child will do all he knows to do with those keys including putting it in his mouth. He is not thinking about the purpose of the keys and all that is attached with it including being able to drive around to different places or getting into car accidents if he is not careful. That child does not know how to drive or even understand the rules of the road. Can you imagine what would happen if that child was told to put the keys in the ignition and drive? It would be a disaster or even death! "When we don't know the purpose of a thing, abuse is inevitable." It is imperative that we not only understand who created sex but also its purpose. For that, we need to go directly to the Source.

The Lord created sex for us to enjoy in the realm of marriage. Sex was created for a married couple to enjoy, connect, and bond with one another. Spiritually it joins two souls and makes them one. It is a vehicle for not only pleasure but to give life, to continue on a legacy, and to birth the next generation. It was created to be enjoyed legally between a husband and his wife. So what happens when we have a generation of unmarried youth or single adults engaging in sex? It opens the door to a host of issues including **broken relationships, multiple sex partners, STD's (some curable others not), HIV/AIDS, abortions, unplanned pregnancies, single parenting, depression, substance abuse** and this list can go on and on. I often wonder: if individuals waited until marriage to have sex and remained monogamous in their marriages, would we have such a widespread of STDS and HIV? Would there be such an increase in abortions? Would there be so many single parent homes? Would the divorce rate be as high as it is? These are all food for thought. This is an example of something good being abused or not used appropriately and, in turn, creating something unhealthy or in some cases destructive.

Exercise

1. When you think about sex, what are the first 5 things that come to mind?

_____

_____

_____

_____

2. Where and from whom did you learn about sex?

_____

_____

_____

_____

3. Do you think it is realistic to wait until marriage for sex? Explain.

_____

_____

_____

_____

Looking Through a Spiritual Lens

'And the two shall become one flesh.' So they are no longer two but one flesh.
(Mark 10:8, ESV)

The sex act is not only physical, mental, and emotional but also spiritual. Something takes place in the spiritual realm when two individuals connect in such an intimate way. When you look at the earliest couples in the Bible, you do not hear about an actual marriage ceremony. It's usually the sex act that connects the couple or consummate the marriage. The Bible states that the two flesh become one. This leads me to believe that there is something very powerful that takes place when a couple has sex. There's also a joining of soul that happens when two individuals have sex. The act leads to two souls coming together as one. This is beautiful for the married couple who wants to be connected. What about the single couples who are engaging in casual sex? What about the one-night stands, booty calls, and hit it and quit it situations? Does the reason for having sex change or influence what happens spiritually (the two flesh becoming one)? And what happens when you are no longer having sex with that person and decide to have sex with someone else? Are you still joined to your previous sex partner? These questions are in order as we further investigate the matter.

I learned about soul ties several years ago. Prior to that, I never even thought about what happened sexually beyond the surface. All I knew was there were sexual relationships that I could not seem to walk away from nor let go of, even when I knew it was not good for me. There were other relationships that even though they had been terminated for years, I couldn't seem to completely shake or stop thinking about them. Was this just because I had a hard time letting go, or was it because there was something deeper going on that I was not aware of? As time went on, the story of the Samaritan woman at the well (John 4:4-30) became significant to me. She was not married, but the Lord told her that she had five husbands and that the man she was currently living with was not her husband. Why would the Lord refer to these men in her past as her husbands if she was not legally married to them? It had to be more than her just living with them that qualified them to be her husband; it had to be the act of sex that qualified them as being married.

Soul ties are formed in many ways and not all of them are unhealthy. As we saw above, a soul tie is created between a husband and his wife with the benefit and purpose of drawing them closer together. There are also ungodly soul ties that can be formed. These soul ties are created when we have sex with multiple partners we are not married to. Unless the soul tie is broken through acknowledgment, repentance, and prayer, we can go through our whole life being connected to people spiritually that we aren't even aware of. This is not to mention also being connected to the people they slept with (WHOA!). We may think we are single and unmarried waiting and believing God for a spouse, but in His eyes, we could also have three, or four, or ten wives or husbands. Believe me, I have had my come to Jesus moment when I had to literally write down the names of the people who I had been intimate with and ask the Lord to break every ungodly soul tie that was formed through fornication between myself and that individual. It was not until I got to that point that I was able to really leave the past behind and shut the door for good on old relationships.

Exercise

1. How many people have you had sex with and what thoughts come to mind?

_____

_____

_____

_____

2. Do you still think about them or feel connected to any of them?

_____

_____

_____

_____

3. If you could do it all over again, what changes (if any) would you make?

_____

_____

_____

_____

Just What Is Sexual Purity?

Flee sexual immorality. Every sin that a man does is outside the body, but he who commits sexual immorality sins against his own body.
(1 Corinthians 6:18, NKJV)

Before we go any further, let's stop and take a look at what sexual purity is. Sexual purity means making a decision to abstain from any form of sexual activity until marriage. Sexual purity looks different for different individuals. It can be identified as no kissing in a courtship or while dating; setting limits on the type of kissing (peck on the lips vs peck on the cheek vs tongue or no tongue involvement); avoiding masturbation, petting and/or stimulating body parts only; setting limits on and placing boundaries around time spent alone with a potential suitor; abstaining from sexual images, music, and messages. It can also include no longer watching your favorite television show where the cast mates are having sex or having sexual intimacy. Side note: one of my favorite shows back in the day was the series "Soul Food" on *Showtime*. My Lord, that was my show. I literally rushed home on Sundays to see what Lem and Bird were up to; Lem was that fine bad boy who some of us seem to like at one point in our lives. Those sex scenes in "Soul Food" were raw and in living color!How in the world did I expect to maintain sexual purity while taking those scenes in week after week, year after year? There was no way that I could! During that time of my life, sexual purity was nowhere on my radar. Thus, sexual purity goes far beyond an act of not having sex while single; it also includes refraining from everything that can arouse or influence one's sexual desires.

Now if you have attended church or have parents or family members who believe in the Lord, I am sure that you have heard that sex before marriage, aka fornication, is a sin. That's mostly what I heard in the church growing up. I did not hear anything else, not even how to abstain; everyone was just focused on telling us not to have sex. If the truth is told, singles in the church were having sex just as much as singles outside of the church. And, to be more honest, married individuals were having sex with singles in and out of the church. There was no true difference with what was happening sexually amongst people in or outside of the church. By the time I started engaging in sex, I honestly believed that the Lord knew it was too hard to abstain from sex and was okay with me having sex. It also seemed as if everyone was doing it, and if not, they wanted to do it. I knew very few virgins during this time and many of them were plotting and planning on the right time to "give it up." Because of what I saw around me, my defense was, God knows my heart. He knows that I can't stop and that made it okay. Besides, I wanted to make sure I knew what I was doing and have some experience for my husband. (Chile, bye. That's one of the devil's lies.) But I really felt that way. The bottom line was, I enjoyed what I was doing and did not want to stop.

A couple of years later, I met a co-worker who was a virgin and who decided to wait until marriage before having sex. She invited me to a "Worth the Wait" program at her church led by Dr. Lindsay Marsh (at the time) and now Warren. She was a 29-year-old virgin waiting on God to get married before she had sex. I was blown away by her testimony and the testimony of others who were a part of the "I am Worth the Wait Revolution." That night changed my life. I ended up purchasing Dr. Lindsay's book, *The Best Sex of my Life: A Guide to Purity,* and it was an eye opener. The biggest take away from her book was that there were people who were being bold and vocal about their stance on waiting for marriage before having sex. The fact that this lifestyle of abstaining from sex could be possible because there were people who were actually living it was mind-boggling to me. Now to be honest, although it would be years until I actually committed to sexual purity, it definitely planted within me the seeds that were needed.

It was the first time that I saw single Christians making a verbal stance and committing to waiting until marriage to have sex. To add to that, these were good looking people. I looked on the stage and I saw both men and women who were standing up and making this verbal commitment in front of everyone. Wow! That's the first time since 7th grade that I actually believed that maybe I could go back to abstaining from sex. That day I went up for prayer and with tears in my eyes, I allowed the ministers to pray for me. The tears came because even though the act of sex was enjoyable in the moment, there was so much that came with it that was unexplainable. There was a feeling of emptiness afterward, a feeling of vulnerability after being with a guy not knowing if he would now act differently because we had sex; that is, not knowing if he would now lose interest and move on to the next person. It's just a lot that comes mentally and emotionally with sex that people are not being honest about. The television shows are not honest about it and neither are the love songs in the music.

Exercise

1. What are your current sexual struggles?

_____

_____

_____

_____

2. What are your personal boundaries when it comes to maintaining sexual purity?

_____

_____

_____

_____

3. What steps will you put in place to ensure that you are able to maintain your personal boundaries?

_____

_____

_____

_____

Wise as a Serpent, Harmless as a Dove

Behold, I send you forth as sheep in the midst of wolves: be therefore wise as serpents, and harmless as doves.
(Matthew 10:16, KJV)

To maintain sexual purity, we must know our triggers and our vices. We have to be transparent. If you know you cannot handle seeing people make-out on that television show, you need to just turn the channel. If you like being around her but notice that every time you get around her, you find yourself thinking about what she would be like in bed or getting hard (let's keep it real), you may need to stay away from her for awhile. If every time you hear that song, your heart starts pounding fast and you find yourself thinking about how he smelled and looked when he was holding you, just turn it off and quick! You may also need to go for a walk, pick up the Word, or call your prayer partner! Do whatever it takes to get your mind back to a peaceful state. Some of you may say it does not take all that. The truth is, it may not. However, for some, it may take all of that and then some. You have to know who you are and what excites you. No one can know that but you.

It took some time for me to learn my triggers and vices. I am the type of person who loves to reminisce. Certain sights and sounds can bring me right back to a place emotionally and physically. Certain music, especially 90's R&B, can really get me so worked up and excited that at times I feel like fainting (Yes, fainting, because I'm so worked up). I have had to learn to just turn it off. Most times I can turn it off and walk away. Sometimes, I pray in the Spirit. Sometimes, I end up listening to it. My prayer is always, 'Lord, please just protect my spirit.' Sometimes, He allows me to listen and when He does, He also tells me when to turn it off. I bring this up to say: this is a journey and a battle. It is a choice that has to be made daily. Every day I make a choice to maintain my sexual purity and that goes far beyond just not having sex. It's a lifestyle. It's a mentality. It's a way of life. It is a journey. Everyone may not choose to live this way, but finding like-minded individuals who have decided to take this path and aligning yourself with them can be a great help.

Exercise

1. What are your all time top 3 favorite songs?

_____

_____

_____

_____

2. Pick one of the 3 songs and pull up the lyrics to that song. What is the message that the writer or singer of the song conveying?

_____

_____

_____

_____

3. Does this song help you to maintain your sexual purity or influence you to think sexual thoughts?

_____

_____

_____

_____

Virginity and Purity

But put on the Lord Jesus Christ, and make no
provision for the flesh, to gratify its desires.
(Romans 13:14, ESV)

If you are still a virgin and are living your life with sexual purity, you deserve to be celebrated! Isn't it crazy how the world will flip that decision to make a person feel offbeat or weird if that person is still a virgin? You are looked at as odd or as if something is wrong with you. Be proud of yourself and your decision to wait, and thank God for keeping you. I believe once we truly know our value and worth, we will not be so quick to give away something that is so valuable and to others who do not deserve it. Some of the things that you do not have to worry about are having a child out of wedlock, receiving an STD, dealing with multiple sex partners, and creating unwanted soul ties. To walk out your decision daily you have to be on guard including being aware of what you allow your senses to take in, monitoring who you spend your time with, and spending time with people who are like-minded. There are hosts of organizations and communities that you can be a part of where you can meet individuals who will provide support and encourage you daily. Community is very important!

Virginity is sacred and a price tag cannot be placed on it. Once it's gone, it's gone forever. You want to make sure that you are giving this sacred gift to your spouse, someone who will value your decision and can and will cherish you because of it. Being a virgin eliminates the comparison game and allows you to be better able to accept the person whom you have said, "I do" to. The comparison game is nothing to take lightly. There are many people who lost out on a good thing because they could not accept who they had in front of them because that person was not like "John" or like "Karen." The Lord may have never wanted you with John or Karen, but because you joined yourself to them through sex, a soul tie was created and now everyone is measured to the likes of John or Karen. The one whom God has approved for you could be sitting right in front of you, but you can't even see him or her because you are looking for the familiar, the traits and personality of John and Karen. It's deep, far deeper than we like to admit or realize.

When I was in the stage of assessing whether or not I wanted to abstain from sex until marriage, I saw a study online showing that couples who waited until marriage to have sex had a healthier sex life and engaged in more sex than couples who had sex prior to marriage. Whether you were a believer in Christ or not and decided to wait, the payoff was still the same: the couple engaged in a more active and enjoyable sex life. That was definitely a plus. One concern that I had was the possibility of the risk of taking a chance on marrying someone who would not measure up sexually based on my experiences from the past (there goes that comparison mentality again). In my mind, I had to know in advance what I was working with because if it was not "good," I would not waste my time. The Lord and I had to work some things out because this was a real concern of mine. The more I developed an intimate relationship with Christ the more I began to trust Him. The more I began to trust Him the more I believed He would not withhold any good thing from me and would take care of even this area of my life because it was a concern for me. I had to go back to the Source (Christ).

I had to remember that the Lord created sex and He created it for our pleasure. My prayer changed to: 'Lord, as I commit myself to doing things Your way, including waiting until marriage to have sex or becoming a born-again virgin, I trust that You will take care of me and ensure that my future spouse and I will have great sex and will satisfy each other.' I even asked the Lord to take away the memories from the past and wipe my slate clean so that we can have a fresh start when the time comes for marriage. I had to remember that the Lord knows me intimately. As a matter of fact, He knows me better than I even know myself. He knows my future spouse as well. He brought our first lady, Eve, to Adam after he custom-made her out of his rib. I had to get to the point where I could surrender my heart's desire to Him and trust that He would take care of even this area of my life. So to my virgins out there: you are to be commended; continue to trust God and lean on Him for support. I pray that the Lord will give you the grace and fortitude to continue to stand true to your convictions with obedience to Him. Know with surety that you will be rewarded and blessed for your efforts.

Exercise

1. Do you believe that it is realistic to maintain your virginity?

_____

_____

_____

_____

2. Why do you think our culture pushes and advertise sex as much as it does?

_____

_____

_____

_____

3. Why is virginity important?

_____

_____

_____

_____

Do Not Give Dogs
What Is Sacred

Do not give dogs what is sacred; do not throw your pearls to pigs. If you do, they may trample them under their feet, and turn and tear you to pieces.
(Matthew 7:6, NIV)

If you found a rare and precious pearl on the side of the road and got it appraised and you learned that it was worth millions, how would you take care of that precious jewel? Would you treat it the same as jewelry that you purchased from the local gas station? I believe it's safe to say that we all know the answer to that question. We **are** that precious jewel. Our value is worth more than we have yet to comprehend. It's easy to say we love ourselves, but the way we really feel about ourselves is shown in the way we treat others or allow ourselves to be treated by others. We are our brother's keeper. Now, this goes beyond me. I have a responsibility to not only maintain sexual purity for myself but to not tempt or become a stumbling block to my brother. Honestly, I could not even focus on the latter until I was able to get control of myself by realizing my own value and worth.

There was a period of my life when I was always referred to as sexy and I loved it. Then I came to a point where I began to think, *hum . . . why am I always referred to as sexy? What is it about me that gives off sex?* As I became more settled in maintaining sexual purity the comments turned from sexy to you are a beautiful woman. You know, I like that more. If we are honest with ourselves, ladies, we don't want to only be referred to as sexy. We have so much more to offer than what we look like or how our bodies are shaped. There is a woman behind our outward appearance with feelings and emotions who wants to be loved, respected, valued, and nurtured—a woman who can support you with your vision, help raise your kids, and be an encourager and help in your time of need. Ladies, men are more than just a nice strong physique to lie up against. There's more to him than that nice smile and 6'2" frame. There's a man with needs, vision, strength, purpose, and destiny who also wants to be loved and valued for what he brings to the table and most importantly respected for who he is. There is no other species on this planet that can take the place of a man, hands down! Men, we need you in your rightful position. A man who knows who he is in Christ and knows his value and worth is a king in my eyes.

Exercise

1. What do you see when you look in the mirror?

_____

_____

_____

_____

2. What are your top 3 strengths?

_____

_____

_____

_____

3. What are 3 things that you need to work on?

_____

_____

_____

_____

I'm Waiting Until Marriage, Now What?

Let marriage be kept honorable in every way, and the marriage bed undefiled. For God will judge those who commit sexual sins, especially those who commit adultery.
(Hebrews 13:4, ISV)

I hope by now you have decided or, at least, started to think of a plan on how to maintain sexual purity as a single person. I'm so glad that abstaining from sex until marriage has an end date. Ladies and gentlemen, thank the good Lord above that it won't be like this forever! Marriage is the goal to legally express ourselves to our mates not only mentally and emotionally but also physically, spiritually, and sexually. How awesome it must be to know that you can express yourself and enjoy freely the pleasures of sex without all the shame, worries, and guilt, and to know that you have the green light to move forward to your heart's content. The Lord has said that marriage is honorable in every way and the marriage bed undefiled. Hallelujah!

Do you know that even if you are single right now that you are someone's wife or someone's husband? Becoming marriage-minded or preparing for marriage should not start when you are engaged to be married. It should start right now while you are single. What you do right now as a single person will affect your future spouse. Engaging in multiple sexual relationships will create multiple soul ties. An unplanned pregnancy can be a result of a sexual relationship in addition to an incurable STD which can also be a result of a sexual relationship as a single person. These are things that will greatly change the dynamics of the relationship between you and your future spouse. Now, if this is the case and you have had a child out of wedlock or an incurable STD, know that there is definitely still hope. Despite our choices and decisions, thank the Lord that He is a great God of second chances and can still work things out for our good. A child, despite the circumstances, is still a blessing from the Lord. There are some who have received an incurable STD and worry about whether or not a spouse will still love and accept them. Rest assured that the Lord will still intervene and send a spouse who will love and cherish you. I know of several instances where an individual received an incurable STD prior to marriage, and once it was shared their spouse still accepted them.

My hope is to bring light to these types of situations that can occur when engaging in sexual relationships as a single person. We have to move to the point where we are looking beyond the moment and analyzing the effects of our choices and decisions. These are the issues that are not discussed or mentioned in the top R&B love songs, in the movies, or in our most popular television show. There is just so much that is attached to being sexually active outside of marriage that the Lord never intended for us to go through. I am sure of that because He left us with instruction in His Word so that we can live a victorious life. We may not like His instructions or understand His ways, but He says what He says to give us hope and a great future.

Practicing sexual purity as a single person will also prepare you to be a better mate and spouse in marriage. It gives you the experience to become mature in developing self-control and patience, two skills that I'm sure will be required in marriage. As mentioned earlier, sexual purity is not just a physical act; it is a state of mind and a lifestyle. Think about the spouse who has to go away on business for a couple of weeks or the spouse who becomes sick unexpectedly for a couple of months and because of their sickness is not able to have sex. Automatically that will eliminate lovemaking for a period of time. So although legally you are free to do it, due to life's circumstances you are not able to. The practice in your single life will have hopefully prepared you or made it easier for you to abstain or wait until it's time even within marriage. We don't always understand or may never understand in this life, why the Lord says what He says, but rest assured, His way brings life and hope, peace and joy, safety and fulfillment of purpose and destiny.

We can have fun without having sex or crossing into the sexual zone. Sometimes we are so focused on what we can't do that we forget about all the things that we can do. **We can write a vision and focus on our goals, make a bucket list of things to accomplish, travel, find new hobbies, meet new people, become involved in ministry and volunteer work.** We can take this time to prepare for marriage by first going to the One who created marriage and read what He says on the matter. We can seek out people who have healthy marriages and ask questions and or spend time with them. We can read books and videos that teach on godly marriages. One thing that we should not be doing in this season is being still and doing nothing. This is a period where we can get busy fulfilling our purpose uninterrupted. Take full advantage of this time because if you are married and with children, you may not be able to do certain things or it may become more difficult.

Exercise

1. How can you prepare to be a wife or husband now in your single state?

_____

_____

_____

_____

2. What are 9 characteristics of the fruit of the Spirit?

_____

_____

_____

_____

3. Which area do you need continued work in?

_____

_____

_____

_____

I Am
My Brother's
Keeper

Finally, all of you be of one mind, having compassion for one another; love as brothers, be tenderhearted, be courteous.
(1 Peter 3:8, NKJV)

Can we go back to being transparent again? I, for one, love to look nice and dress nice. I have always been into fashion and bringing my own style to whatever I wear. Let's face it: we all like to look good. We know what our assets are and we know how to play them up when we need to. Being modest in dress does not mean wearing a cape over our bodies. Or wearing long skirts to the ground. It does mean being wise in how we carry ourselves, especially around the opposite sex. For years, I loved to look sexy. I knew what looked right on me and what heels to wear that would add that special kick and I did not feel bad about it. Now that I have committed to sexual purity, I understand that what I wear and how I look can affect the opposite sex. Is my style allowing others to stumble by leading them to think thoughts that only my husband should be thinking about me? Am I showing too much? These things need to be considered when getting dressed. Women, we have the ability to assist a man with his purpose or cause him to stumble. We have to learn how to use our femininity to encourage not hinder. I am responsible for my brother. I want to support him in his walk. And most importantly, because I am someone's wife, I don't want the next man looking at me in a way that would be offensive to my spouse.

Brothers, the same goes for you. Personally, there is nothing better than seeing a man who has a nice rippled body, who smells good and who has a nice smile. Let's be clear: If you are fine you're just fine. However, being mindful how you present yourself towards the opposite sex should be considered. The current trend in male dress is tight fitting jeans or pants and tight shirts. There's so much that can be said here about this style, but I digress. Even though I know that tight clothing (even for men) is the current trend, you have to ask yourself why is it important for people to see everything that you are working with? Or why is it important for me to show others everything that I am working with? The bulge in your pants, the split in your behind—what's going on? In the words of one of the Braxtons: "That's not hot!" Now if I am having a conversation with you and all I can see is your bulge in your pants, do you think that I am actually focused on what you are saying? Maintaining sexual purity is hard enough with all the images being constantly thrown at us on the internet, on the television, on billboards, and in magazines. Brother, if you care about me, help me out and support me in my stance by covering up.

Exercise

1. Do you believe that your actions impact the opposite sex? Explain.

_____

_____

_____

_____

2. What nonverbal messages do you send to the opposite sex?

_____

_____

_____

_____

3. When you are complimented, what phrases do you often hear most?

_____

_____

_____

_____

Getting Busy With My Purpose

'For I know what I have planned for you,' says the
LORD. *'I have plans to prosper you, not to harm you.*
I have plans to give you a future filled with hope.'
(Jeremiah 29:11, NET)

Now that I know the what is and the why's and have determined in my mind to be steadfast in maintaining sexual purity, it's now time to take my focus off of SEX altogether and get busy with my purpose. Yes, let it go. Do you know that the Lord has a unique purpose and plan for your life that only you can fulfill? You have been born for a reason despite life's challenges and circumstances. Despite the many mistakes that you and I have made and sometimes over and over again, we thank the Lord for His grace and mercy. Ask for forgiveness, turn back, and try again. As long as we are living we are prone to sin. However, let's not use that as a crutch or a pathway to continue on in our ways of bondage. It is easier to stop doing something that is not beneficial when we are able to look at the bigger picture. By briefly analyzing the long and short-term effects, we can ask ourselves if our current choices and decisions are bringing us closer to or farther away from our hearts desires or goals? Once examined, we will be more equipped and purposeful in following our goals.

As I reflect on my journey (and what a journey it has been). I can now see how my life experiences have made me into the woman that I am today. Yes, I have gone through some things and have not always chosen wisely, but I am uniquely me. I can now be the example that I was always looking for. I can help the next brother or sister who is on his or her journey to sexual purity without being judgmental or harsh but with love and compassion. Hey, I truly understand. RE-shifting my focus has also helped me tremendously. Let's face it, I can be honest and say that at times (or maybe most of the time), I used sex as medicine to make me feel good. I spent most of my young adult life trying to figure it out, not sure how to get to some of my goals including being a wife instead of a girlfriend. I never even realized that I had to also be the person that I was looking for in a spouse! There were also times that after sex, I would feel so empty and like pieces of me were being chipped away. This act that is made to look so romantic in the movies, in music, and on television shows where people have sex and live happily ever after was really just . . . television.

In real life, this act called sex, although it feels good in the moment, also brings so many issues with it. I remember my old pastor preaching a sermon and mentioning that some of you should have HIV right now **BUT** by the grace of God who stopped it from entering your system. In the act, you were spared! Boy, could I have jumped up and run around the church! That was truth and my truth at its best. I haven't always made the best decisions but still in my sin, God loved me enough to protect me! He really is a loving God who cares deeply for us. This world has a way of glorifying all the things that the Lord despises and casting down all of the things that the Lord cherishes. To be wise, to overcome, to be fulfilled with a fulfillment that premarital sex will not bring, we must go back to God to seek out what our created purpose is. What are those things that make your heart glad? What are those things that you are good at that come effortlessly? What are those things that if you were not afraid to dream you would be doing right now? It's time to wake up, to stop sleepwalking, and to stop wasting precious time that we cannot get back once it's gone.

Brothers, it's time to get back to the basics, back to a place where you understand your value and worth. You were made with such strength and valor. You can change a nation. When you are not in your position the women and children are uncovered and unprotected. Sisters, it's time for us to know our worth and realize the power that we truly possess. One of my old co-workers stated that he blamed women for the way men act now. If we elevated our standards and enforced some boundaries, men would rise to the occasion and meet us where we are instead of giving us anything knowing that we will accept it. And you know, as much as I love to debate, I couldn't even argue with him on that one. It's time for us all to rise and take our rightful position. It's time to be the change that this generation so desperately wants to see. Who will stand up and set the tone? Legacy is waiting. Sexual purity until marriage is one way of ensuring that our families will not be broken, and thus, remain intact.

Exercise

1. What are you most passionate about?

_____

_____

_____

_____

2. **If money or age was not an issue,** what would you do right now?

_____

_____

_____

_____

3. What is your purpose? (If you don't know, you may need to spend some time in prayer and fasting.) Write down what the Lord shares with you.

_____

_____

_____

_____

Hiding Behind My Truth for Abstinence

And ye shall know the truth,
and the truth shall make you free.
(John 8:32)

By now you may have picked up on my heart for transparency. I just don't know how else to live. As the words of Usher's song "Truth Hurts" comes to mind, I also think about the Scripture that says the truth shall set you free. I struggled tremendously with abstinence. It always seemed like I could not make it past the one year mark and in that season, there were a lot of things that I could not see. When you are in it, sometimes it's hard to connect the dots. The Lord then showed me the timing of my decision to going back to abstinence. It was usually at the end of a relationship. It seemed like when I was alone, I was cool; but when I entered into a relationship everything that I stood for or desired went right out the window. And you know, although I said I wanted to be abstinent because I wanted to do things the Lord's way, I lied. I was lying to myself and to God. Well, He knew the truth. Further exploration and frustration would eventually show me different.

My choice of abstinence in certain moments of my life came from a place of hurt and not wanting to be bothered. Not wanting to be touched. Not wanting to give another piece of myself away period. It really had nothing to do with being obedient to God. It usually came into play after a breakup from a relationship that I knew I really had no business being in to begin with. It was like I was a walking contradiction when it came to romantic relationships. I said I wanted to be married to a man who loved the Lord, but I advertised myself as a party girl just wanting to have fun. Looking back, I realized that I picked a reflection of who I really was and where I really was at the time. And because I was broken I could only identify with men who were also broken: men, like myself, who did not want to do the work that it took to deal with some things, so they instead, took the time to perfect the thing that gave them temporary relief and joy; that is, sex.

I will admit that I was one who used sex for medicine. It made me feel good. It made me feel better. It was a distraction from me and the work that I needed to do to get to the place I needed to be. So in my young adulthood, I spent a lot of time looking good, being in shape, wearing the right clothes—just being sexy. I got tattoos that were sexy and even a belly piercing. Hearing a guy say, 'Girl, you are SEXY' was everything. All of my efforts went into crafting a certain outward appearance. I was so busy crafting an outward appearance that I never took the time to deal with the internal stuff, never mind the woman who was crying on the inside because she felt so empty and so alone, so misunderstood. Instead of identifying the source of the problem, I medicated it.

I can't remember when the Lord connected the dots for me, but in His perfect timing, He eventually opened my eyes of understanding so I could really see myself, and not the person that I portrayed myself to be in public, but the person who when no one was around had a hard time sleeping through the night, especially with the lights off and who needed the distraction of the noise from the television so that I could not hear my own true thoughts knocking on my heart. And no matter how tired I was, the Lord continued to wake me up at certain times in the morning, namely, 1 a.m. and 3 a.m. At those times, all I could do was open the Bible and lay it on my chest until I fell back to sleep. After all, I heard the preacher at church say that the Word was alive—that it was a living Word. I trusted that it could help me, somehow.

As the Lord opened my eyes, He showed me that my desire for abstinence, although I told the world that it was out of wanting to do things God's way, was really because I had nothing left to give in that moment, and that was why I was not successful at it. I usually fell right back into having sex when the hurt was no longer visible and when the pain was no longer on the surface. At that point, I ran back to what was familiar, what was comfortable. I thank the Lord that He showed me this fact. I had no clue that that was hidden in my heart. I had to stop and lay it out before the Lord asking

Him to show me what my true intentions were, why I was not successful at abstinence, and what was really going on with me. After He showed me, I asked Him to help me to get to where I needed to be. I had to be honest and explore whether or not I really wanted to be abstinent and what was my reason for it. I decided I wanted to wait for marriage before engaging in sex because I was worth more than giving myself to someone in such an intimate way who was not my husband. Sex complicated things and it blurred my vision to thinking clearly and making wise decisions in selecting a mate. Finally, I wanted to remain abstinent because I trusted that God's way was best for me. Sex is His design and His creation that should be used in the way He intended it to be used. I decided that I would lean on Him for help and guidance and no longer try to do things in my own strength.

Exercise

1. Is your decision to remain abstinent rooted in fear? Explain.

_____

_____

_____

_____

2. Pray and ask the Lord to reveal whatever may be hidden in your heart. What did He reveal to you?

_____

_____

_____

_____

3. What steps will you take to deal with it?

_____

_____

_____

_____

8 Practical Steps Towards Sexual Purity

Ask, and it will be given to you; seek, and you will find; knock, and it will be opened to you.
(Matthew 7:7, NKJV)

Sexual purity is not only a process but a choice that you make daily. It's a decision to walk a path that is not popular. It's a path that may close many doors to you and may, at times, seem harder to find the open doors. However, if you decide to take this path, it is a road that eliminates many heartaches and pains, it eliminates building unhealthy soul ties, and it excludes the need of worry about receiving an STD or unplanned pregnancy. It empowers you to make healthy choices and decisions and allows you to hear the Lord's voice clearly without distraction. Last, it allows you to get busy living on purpose for what the Lord has called you to do. Here are 8 practical steps that you can take to help you along the way.

1. Make a decision on whether you want to maintain sexual purity or not.

You are the only person who can make this decision. It can't be based on what the pastor says is the right thing to do or about what your parents have told you to do. You have to count the cost for yourself and decide if this is something that is of value or worth to you.

2. Decide what sexual purity means to you.

A great starting point would be to read the Bible and find out what it says about sexual purity. Although these words are not specifically in the Bible, the Word talks about fleeing sexual immorality and fornication. There is a due diligence of a single believer in Christ to be holy as Christ is holy and this includes not awakening love before its time.

3. Know your true intentions for wanting to live with sexual purity.

If you have decided to maintain sexual purity until marriage you must know what is driving your decision. In some cases, you may be very clear; in others, you may not know. In both cases, ask the Lord to show you what is hidden in your heart; that is, what might be driving your decision to be abstinent that you might not be aware of. Once this is revealed allow the Lord to help you to do the work. The irony is, many times you find that fear of some sort is sometimes driving a person's decision to be abstinent.

4. Know your vices and triggers.

This is a key step and one that you must be aware of to be successful. Being aware of what stimulates your five senses and what is a turn on to you is a must! I think of Shakespeare's quote: "To thine own self be true." We have to move from being unaware to being aware. Once we are aware, we can be on guard to the things that we allow in our senses through music and media. We have to be more selective about the company we keep and even of the places that may now be off limits. Once you know your vices, you are able to set realistic boundaries in your life.

For me to be successful, I have had to know my limits. The truth is, there are just some conversations that I just can't have anymore. And yes, I am grown, but there are certain shows on the television that I just can't watch. R&B 90's music is something that I absolutely love but most songs I just can't handle; they over-stimulate me. I have to set boundaries in my relationships with the opposite sex. I have to be honest with myself that even though I am attracted to an individual (sexually or physically), and yes, even though he is my brother in Christ and I should be able to hang out with him, I just might not be able to in a one-to-one setting. Again, it may not take all that for you, but I have to be aware of who I am. Know your triggers.

5. Identify an accountability partner.

If we are honest with ourselves, no matter how old we are, it is comforting knowing that someone has our back. It is comforting knowing that there is someone out there who is willing to support us and is open to taking the time to invest in helping us reach our goals. Identifying an accountability partner is imperative. This needs to be someone you trust, feel comfortable with, and can be transparent with. It has to be someone who you know will take what you are asking of them seriously and someone who will really hold you accountable. This is especially important once you have met a potential mate during the courting/dating phase. An accountability partner can play a significant role in helping you set boundaries.

One thing to also consider when identifying an accountability partner is to make sure that this person also agrees with sexual purity and is also or has also lived their life with this value.

6. Surround yourself with like-minded individuals / support groups.

Support. Support. Support. Can you see the trend? We just can't be successful in this Christian walk much less maintain sexual purity living on an island by ourselves. My decision to maintain sexual purity came at a time when I was not connected to a church home much less connected to people who wanted to live the same way that I chose to live. I really had to stay in prayer and search for what I was looking for. The Bible says that we are to work out our own salvation with fear and trembling (Philippians 2:12). Finding organizations that promote sexual purity, books and videos that support maintaining sexual purity is a must. Once I found out about "Worth the Wait Revolution," I followed the organization online to get as much information as I could.

Today, there are a lot of organizations that have taken a stance of sexual purity. You can find them by doing a Google search. It is fair to say that even in your church family or community, there may not be many people who are at the place of choosing sexual purity for their lives. They just may not be at that point yet or have decided not to walk on this path. As a result, there may not be any peers readily available to partner with. The Lord may be calling **YOU** to be the change that you want to see around you. Do not be afraid. If the Lord has placed an urging in your heart to walk on this path, trust and know that at the appointed time, He will provide you with all the resources that you need.

7. Pray without ceasing.

Pray, pray, pray all day every day. Prayer is a must. The truth is we just can't do this in our own strength. We need the Holy Spirit to give us power to stand in a day and time where a sexual agenda is being pushed in the world. Understand that this is not a coincidence that you can't turn on the television without seeing someone dressed provocative, making out, or having sex. And if these three things are not happening, they are talking about one of these three things. We are in a spiritual battle and there is an enemy who plans to steal, kill, and destroy. Prayer is your weapon to stand. Prayer opens the doors to the resources that you need. Prayer gives you strength to continue on when you feel weak. Prayer provides the right support around you in due season. Prayer allows you to hear confidently the Lord's will for your life.

8. Get busy living on purpose.

Now that I have decided to take a stand and keep myself sexually pure until marriage, I'm armed with support and prayer; it's now time to take my mind off of sex and get busy living with purpose. As I have moved forward with praying and fasting about what the Lord wanted me to do during this single season of my life, He made alive in me many passions and interests. Some interests I didn't know was there, and some I had not tapped into for years. It's amazing how the Lord brings it all together and does not waste anything. He uses every experience and passion that we have to not only help us but to help others and for His glory. Living a life of sexual purity does not have to be boring and neither does it have to be a life of hiding in your house from fear of slipping up. It can be fun, full of laughter, exploring and discovering new things and meeting new people (one of who can be a potential mate).

I love to travel (having visited over ten Caribbean islands to date). I now want to travel to new places (Italy, Australia, South Africa, London). I love to create and that includes crocheting and sewing clothes. (Although I'm no longer focused on looking sexy all the time, I still love fashion and unique clothing.) I love to cook and try new recipes including coming up with tasty and healthy meals, and making cakes and pastries from scratch. I love to write and I ended up creating 2 blogs, and now I'm writing my first book on something that came so natural due to my life experiences and help from the Holy Spirit. I created a Christian business for girls called LOIE (Lady of Integrity and Excellence). Its purpose is to help young ladies with practical steps to live righteously in their everyday lives. This organization was birthed out of my own pain, frustrations, and experiences.

Do you see how every skill and talent can be used interconnectedly with living on purpose? All the things that the Lord has called me to do during this season of my life have really come effortlessly because it was already inside of me. I see now how every step has been ordered by the Lord. The best part is that there is now no guilt and condemnation associated with it. I can go to sleep and wake up in peace. I look and feel less stressed. Take this time to explore and get busy with all that the Lord has called you to do! I'm sure that you will be filled with more joy than you have yet to experience.

I've Slipped Up, Now What?

If you have slipped up in any way, start over. Go through these steps again. Analyze what area is lacking and put some additional effort and support in it. Increase your prayer time and be intentional about pursuing the Lord for guidance. This journey is a process and I can relate first hand that it took time to get here. Once I engaged in these 8 practical steps, it became much easier for me to live with sexual purity. Please do not allow condemnation and guilt to keep you down and off-track. Repent, turn back and continue to move forward.

Moving Forward

Brethren, I do not count myself to have apprehended;
but one thing I do, forgetting those things which are
behind and reaching forward to those things which are
ahead. I press toward the goal for the prize of the
upward call of God in Christ Jesus.
(Philippians 3:13-14, NKJV)

As you take this journey of maintaining sexual purity until marriage, I challenge you to spend some time with the Lord asking Him to reveal to you any hidden agendas that you might have. Ask Him to show you what's really hidden in your heart and pray for strength and courage to deal with the real issues. I pray that He will give you the grace to go through the process without condemnation because it is a process. Some people have maintained their virginity. Some people have been having sex for years and may now decide to stop while others may have been on this abstinence path for years. Where ever you are, know that the Lord will meet you right where you are.

My journey was a process of trial and error even after I received the revelation from the Lord of my real initial reason of wanting to be abstinent. I ended up in another sexual relationship for a period of two years: one year of being in the relationship and another year of trying to get out of it. That soul tie was serious! But for the first time, I started to really feel convicted about having sex and continuing on in my relationship with the Lord. This was new and something that I had never felt before. I prayed and asked the Lord daily to help me get out of this relationship. It did not happen overnight, but the Lord definitely gave me the strength to walk away. And I have not looked back since. Yes, it's a daily decision to maintain sexual purity until marriage, but it is something that I take great joy in doing. Every day the Lord builds my confidence in Him, in His power, and in His strength. I am a testament that the Lord is a keeper; if you want to be kept, He will keep you from falling.

I want to make it clear that just because this has been my personal life experience, I am by no means an expert. Every day, I have to choose to live life God's way. I have to premeditate my day. I have to examine closely who I will hang around and spend time with and who will I call a "friend." I examine whose phone call I will take (just because the phone rings does not mean you have to answer). There are certain guys who I find myself sexually attracted to and in those cases, I limit the contact and keep it on a hi and bye basis. I take the time to examine what I wear to work, church, and other settings. If I find myself second guessing as to whether or not it's too revealing or showing too much, I just take it off and try again. When it comes to music, I still limit what I listen to, and for a person who loves good music and who loves to dance this area can be challenging. My point is, this is not a one-time deal. Every day I have to take steps to continue on the path that I am on now. I have to trust God, and pray and ask for His help continually. I have to do something. Sexual purity is not maintained without some level of sacrifice, but looking at the bigger picture, the end results make it worth it.

At the end of the day, I look forward to experiencing sex the way that God invented it, not what man has reinvented. I am excited. I know in God's perfect timing, in my season of marriage, not only will it be a God-honoring union, but it will be one filled with great sex free from fear, guilt, and condemnation. I can't do anything else but smile at the Lord and thank Him for loving us so much and for creating something so great to be experienced here on this earth.

Lord, I just thank You today that You are a God of second chances. Thanks for never turning Your back on me and abandoning me along the way despite my ways that were not pleasing to You. Thank You, Jesus, that Your ways are greater than our ways, and today, I choose to follow You.

Suffering from Sexual Abuse

A couple months after the writing of this book, the Lord laid it on my heart to add a section on sexual abuse, molestation, rape, and incest. This topic can be a difficult one to discuss and many people prefer to sweep it under the rug for various reasons. A few reasons are: some who were violated believe that it was their fault. They believe that they did something to deserve the violation. There is a lot of self-blame, which often leads to shame, guilt, denial, or depression. It's time for us to start discussing these difficult issues and stop shying away from having these hard conversations. Sexual abuse unchecked can lead to serious implications in the victims' lives. It will impact their relationships with others, their view of themselves, and can lead to trust issues. Sexual abuse unchecked can also create unhealthy soul ties that can affect a person way into that person's marriage.

Wikipedia defines **sexual abuse**, also referred to as molestation, as forcing undesired **sexual** behavior by one person upon another. When that force is immediate, of short duration, or infrequent, it is called **sexual** assault. This is a direct violation of how the Lord wants sex to be used. Sexual abuse can occur between married and unmarried individuals.

According to the Bureau of Justice Statistics' National Criminal Victimization Survey, in 2012, there were 346,830 reported rapes or sexual assaults of persons 12 years or older. [Truman, J., L. Langton, and M. Planty, "Criminal Victimization 2012," U.S. Department of Justice, Office of Justice Programs, Bureau of Justice Statistics, October 2013. (http://www.bjs.gov/content/pub/pdf/cv12.pdf) (February 19, 2014)]

Being a victim of sexual abuse will distort and impact your vision of sex whether it's realized or not. It can also leave deep-seated scars. My prayer is that everyone who has been a victim of sexual abuse, molestation, rape, or incest will decide to deal with it today.

I pray that you will allow the Lord to heal you of the scars and that you will not allow what happened to you to define who you are or hold you back from the person God has created you be. Some are angry with the Lord and have asked, Lord, why would You allow this to happen to me? Please know that what happened to you was never the Lord's plan for you. We live in a fallen world where people are influenced by the powers of darkness, where bad choices and decisions are made daily. We live in a world where the Lord has given us all a free will and because of that, bad things happen to us at the hands of others. In spite of that, be assured that the

Lord wants to heal our broken hearts, heal the wounds and scars, and help us to overcome. He will even help you to forgive the perpetrator. He will also help you to forgive yourself even if you were the perpetrator. Forgiveness and confession are key to true healing from the inside out.

There are instances where people who have been sexually abused or violated are now abstinent and believe that they are abstaining from sex because of their vow of celibacy to the Lord. However, because of the violation, it has made them shut down and not want to be bothered. So although they are being obedient to the Lord's will of abstaining from fornication, it's not for the right reason. It's imperative to know why we are making the choices that we are making because if it is unchecked we can be living in a pattern of waiting or on hold because of fear. On the opposite extreme, individuals who have been sexually abused or violated may become sexually promiscuous. They may find themselves unable to stop engaging in sex almost to a point where they feel like something is driving them. They may want to stop but can't. They have limited control over their flesh. In these instances, transparency is key. Talk to a pastor, therapist, or loved one—someone you can trust to discuss the violation. Ask the Lord to help you to overcome. In most cases, the soul tie created in the act has to be broken (please see the soul tie prayer).

There are no easy answers and solutions to being violated and abused in this way. Healing is a process. Talking about it is a great first step. Talking also takes away the shame and the guilt. The enemy is no longer able to hurl ongoing accusations because it is no longer a secret as it has been exposed. Trust

God. He's not the enemy. He cares and He knows and wants to help you to overcome. Ask Him to heal the hurt, the pain, and the disappointment. Ask Him to teach you how to trust again. He will. When you are ready, share your story and testimony as you being able to overcome will help the next person who currently feels stuck. Your voice, your story, your experience when shared with others will impact many. Someone out there is waiting to hear your story, and how you overcome will give them hope to believe that they, too, can also overcome.

My prayer is that if you have been violated in any way by the same sex or opposite sex through sexual abuse, violation, rape, or incest that you do not allow the experience to hinder you from living the life that you deserve. You are not damaged goods. That's a lie from the enemy. There is a godly husband or wife out there who will love and value you. All men and women are not out to harm you. You are lovable. The Lord can restore your natural affections. You don't have to hurt in secret. You can trust again. You can have the love that you want and desire. You can live fear free. You can live a purpose filled life. Talk to someone. Pray to the Lord. Be real with Him and tell Him exactly what's on your heart. Your prayers may be "Lord, I am angry with You for…." Rest assured that the Lord is big enough to handle your anger and frustrations toward Him. He wants to help you. He's waiting on you to be honest with Him so that He can intervene. He knows how you really feel anyway. Just tell Him and let Him heal you. My brother and/or sister know that there is purpose in your pain. God bless you.

Call to Salvation

Do you know with surety where you will spend eternity? This life on earth is temporal. Thank the Lord that He paid the price for all of our sins on the cross. There was not one worthy enough to bear the burdens of this world but Jesus Christ. He came to the earth with the sole purpose of dying for our sins (yours and mine) so that we can have a chance at eternal life. The price is free to all. All we have to do is accept it. If you have not accepted the Lord Jesus Christ as your personal Savior, it is not too late. The Word says that if you confess with your mouth that Jesus Christ is Lord and believe in your heart that God raised Him from the dead, you will be saved (Romans 10:9).

All of these things that we have talked about (maintaining sexual purity and virginity and getting busy with your purpose) cannot be maintained consistently without the help of the Lord. If you will like to accept Him, today, as your personal Savior repeat this prayer with me:

Lord, I am a sinner and there is nothing that I can do to earn my salvation. It is a gift that You have given to me freely. I ask that You forgive me of my sins and I accept You into my heart as my personal Savior. I believe that You died on the cross for my sins and arose again with all power and authority. Lord, I ask You to be the Lord of my life from this day forward. I know that You have created me with a unique purpose and plan despite my past circumstances. Help me to move forward in it. You are the only way to salvation. I welcome You into my heart, today, and thank You for saving me. Amen.

Now that you are saved, your next step will be to continue to build a personal relationship with Jesus through prayer, that is, talking to Him daily, and reading His Word. Find a Bible-believing church where you can connect with like-minded believers who can encourage, teach, and be a support to you in the things of the Lord. The Word says that faith comes by hearing and by hearing the Word of God (Romans 10:17). The more you hear God's Word, the more your faith will grow. I love you and I am praying for you. God bless.

Soul Tie Prayer

Dear Lord, I ask in the name of Jesus that You cut all unhealthy soul ties that have been formed through sex or sexual acts between myself and _____. Bring to my mind every single person who I am in bondage to due to illicit sex. Lord, my desire is to be holy as You are holy and to maintain sexual purity until marriage. I commit my body, mind, and thoughts to You. Restore what has been lost or stolen, in the mighty name of Jesus. Thank You for Your undying love towards me and remind me constantly that there is nothing that I can do to forfeit Your love. In Jesus' name. Amen.

Q & A Section

This section is the Question / Answer section. It is dedicated to questions that you might have after reading this book.

How do you stop having sex when you are in a relationship with someone who wants to continue having sex?

If you have counted the cost of maintaining sexual purity until marriage and have explained to your partner that you have decided to stop and your partner does not feel the same way, the best decision is to walk away from the relationship. I think of the Scripture that says, how can two walk together unless they agree (Amos 3:3). It does not mean that that individual is a bad person; it just means that both of you are not walking on one accord and that's okay. Go in peace.

I am able to stop having sex but can't stop masturbating, what should I do?

Masturbation was hard for me to stop as well. For years, I thought it was harmless and looked at it as "safe sex." The more you read the Word and learn what it says about fleeing sexual immorality, the more you will be able to view it from the Lord's lenses. For me, that brought conviction when I participated in it. Masturbation is something that will fuel your sex drive and make it harder to abstain from sexual thoughts, feelings, and desires. Most times people masturbate to feel better. Getting to the real root of your need for masturbation is key. Are you avoiding, hiding, looking for, or running away from something? Pray and ask the Lord for help.

Is it realistic to be a virgin until marriage?

Yes, it is very realistic. There are many men and women of all different ages who are still virgins who have decided to wait until marriage to have sex. I'm sure that it is not easy. Google search organizations or support groups for individuals who are virgins to build a support network of people who have taken a stand to maintain their virginity.

What about kissing, is that maintaining sexual purity?

Kissing is viewed differently by different individuals. Know your vice and your triggers. I personally love to kiss, but I know that it's a struggle to stop there. I can handle a **peck** on the cheek or **maybe** on the lips, but that's as far as I can go without my mind and body wanting more. Ask yourself:

What is my purpose for kissing? Decide if you will kiss and if so who (boyfriend, fiance?), and when (courtship, engagement, or marriage?), and what type of kissing (peck, tongue or no tongue involvement). It's a personal decision. Some people can handle kissing and are not tempted to go any further. Know your own limits and stick to it.

How do I prepare myself for marriage as a teen?

You prepare yourself for marriage as a teen by believing at this age that you are someone's future husband or wife. How you carry yourself now will impact your mate. Read scripture on marriage and discuss with mentors. Decide what sexual purity means to you. Find a support network or group. If you can't find one create one. Pray and ask the Lord for daily guidance on how to prepare to be a wife, and pray for your future spouse as well.

Am I too young to think about sexual purity?

If you are asking this question, you are not too young. Having a plan at any age is helpful and will keep you on the right path, especially in a world where there are no limits to what you are exposed to through media, television, internet, school, and peers. Talk to your parent or a trusted adult at church for their thoughts and support. The best thing that you can do is talk about it and ask questions.

If I am engaged and about to be married, is it okay to participate in sexual activities with my fiance?

Of course, this is a personal decision and one that you have to count the cost for yourself. Being engaged (and thus not married) and having sex is still fornication. At this point, we should all be clear on the Lord warning us to flee fornication. If you have made it to the engagement period without having sex, great job! If not, you and your fiance can always decide to stop, repent, and ask the Lord for help and seek guidance on how to proceed and abstain until your wedding day. I know it's hard, but it can be done with two people being on one accord and with the Lord's help.

So are you suggesting that I stop listening to music and stop watching television? That seems to be very extreme.

No, I am not suggesting that. One thing is certain, to maintain abstinence and sexual purity you **have** to protect your mind. There is no way around it. Every action starts in the mind. One way that we can guard our mind and protect it from sneak attacks that the enemy sends our way is by knowing our vices and triggers. What gets you excited? What makes you sexually aroused? You have to know this and have a plan in place. For me, I have to limit the types of music that I listen to and what I watch on television. Certain music and lyrics talking about love get me excited. The 90's R&B music is a trigger for me. I do enjoy listening to certain Gospel, jazz, instrumentals, and soft rock music. However, I am now more aware of the lyrics and the words that the singer is singing about. The beat may be hot, but if it is talking about bumping and grinding, it's in my best interest to turn it off. That works for me; you have to set your own limits.

I feel so alone on this journey, like no one understands me and people can hardly relate to me, what should I do?

You know, I can relate to those feelings and to be quite honest with you, those feelings come and go. The truth is, this journey at times can feel lonely especially depending on what we are focusing on. Remember this truth: the Lord said, He will never leave us nor forsake us. So despite feeling alone at times, we know the Lord is right there with us even when we may not feel Him. We are living in a world that is getting darker and darker. A world that holds views that are in direct opposition to God. It sometimes feels like we are standing alone on this path, but that is also a lie despite what we see. There is a remnant of people who are abstaining and who have made the commitment to live for the Lord. Look for support during these times of loneliness. Volunteer. Focus on the bigger picture. Take up a new hobby. Look for organizations in your area that you can be a part of.

Sexual Purity Commitment

I, _____, agree with the Lord and believe that abstaining from fornication is a form of taking care of myself and is in my best interest. I forgive myself for past transgressions and I know that once I confess my sins to the Lord, He will forgive me. I will no longer condemn myself because of my past or allow anyone else to. I am a new creation in Christ Jesus.

- I commit to keeping myself sexually pure until marriage.
- I commit to protecting my ears, eye gates, and conversation from sexual temptation.
- I commit to presenting myself as a child of God at all times.
- I commit to helping my brother and sister by sharing my testimony and advising them without condemning them.

(Signature)_____

(Date)_____

About the Author

Lisa Gordon is originally from Boston, Massachusetts, and is a first-time author. This book was birthed out of her own experiences and lessons she learned. She holds a master's degree from Howard University and is a Licensed Clinical Social Worker who works with high school students in the Washington, DC metropolitan area. Lisa has a passion for truth and a passion to help the younger generation live their life on purpose for the Lord by using practical everyday skills.

Resources

When I was growing up, it was so hard to find the information needed to help me along my path. The onset of the internet brought access to many resources. However, just because it's on the web does not mean that it's truth. Always ask the Lord for wisdom and remember to go back to the Source. With that said, here are some resources that I believe you will find to be valuable for your personal use or to be recommended to others. Also, feel free to email me at LoieLLC@gmail.com with any questions about this book or if you have any prayer needs.

Blogs
Living a Lifestyle of Integrity & Excellence
Loieonpurpose.blogspot.com

Books
The Best Sex of My Life: A Guide to Purity, by Dr. Lindsay Marsh
Those Who Wait on God, by Nicole and Tony Hinton

Websites
Those Who Wait on God, Facebook page
Waiting Till Marriage, www.waitingtillmarriage.org
Abstinence Works, www.abstinenceworks.org
Worth the Wait Revolution, www.iamworththewait.com

YouTube Channnels
Ashley Empowers - Dating with Purpose Series

Acknowledgments

I want to take the time to thank You, Lord, for never leaving my side. You have always been there for me, loving me when I had nothing to give myself. Thank You, Lord, for the many gifts that You have given me and for allowing me to walk into the purpose and plan that You have destined for me.

Lord, I thank You that this book will cross the Atlantic and Pacific oceans and will get into the hands of many internationally who need to hear the contents and testimony of this book. Lord, I thank You that the information that You have given me in this book will break chains and set many free in Jesus' name.

I would also like to thank my parents, my brother, family (Astoria St.), and friends for your love and continued support. Mommy, I thank you for always being there for me and loving me through all of life's ups and downs. I can always depend on you and thank God for you! Thank You, Lord, for my church family: Pastor Dale and First Lady, who have taken the time to disciple and plant seeds that are growing in my life; Minister Belinda and Evangelist Lennett who loved me unconditionally; and every member of DC City Church who accepted and loved me just the way I am. Special thanks to Minister Bacon, for speaking a word to me after Bible study that released me to start writing this book that night!

46490837R00066

Made in the USA
Middletown, DE
01 August 2017